LET'S TALK ABOUT IT:

Extraordinary Friends

FRED ROGERS

PHOTOGRAPHS BY JIM JUDKIS

G. P. PUTNAM'S SONS

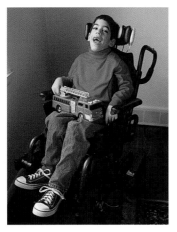

Josh likes fire trucks, trains, race cars, cats, horseback riding, swimming, visiting people, pizza, and jokes!

Sam likes to ice skate, read books with lots of facts and figures, eat pizza and spaghetti, perform magic tricks, and tell jokes!

Tori G. likes to play dress-up, build with Duplo blocks, and play with dolls. She likes French fries and hot dogs.

Tori N. likes to play dress-up, eat potato chips, play with her rabbit, "Hopscotch," ride her bike, and swim.

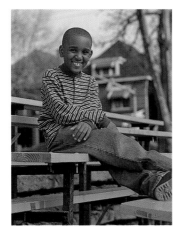

Shawn likes to go to the Boys and Girls Club after school with Xavier. He also likes football, baseball, hot dogs, and pizza.

Xavier likes to play outside, especially baseball with Shawn. He likes to eat pizza and his "Grandma's chunky cinnamon applesauce."

A friend once gave me a piece of calligraphy which I've kept in my office ever since. It's a quotation from *The Little Prince* by Antoine de St. Exupéry which reads: "L'Essentiel est invisible pour les yeux." ("What is essential is invisible to the eye.") Those may seem like unexpected words to find in the office of a person who works in such a visual medium as television, but I find the truth of those words growing deeper within me every day.

When we see someone who looks or behaves differently from what's familiar to us, it's possible to feel a little shy, scared, curious, or awkward. I know how much I've struggled to look with my heart and not with just my eyes when I see someone who is obviously different from me. If adults have such a challenge, imagine what a challenge that can be for children.

Some children and families have bridged that gap, and we have enjoyed sharing their extraordinary friendships through this book. It certainly was obvious to us that such relationships bring benefits to everyone.

Whether or not you know someone with a disability, we hope this book will be of help to you as you talk with your child about how people are alike and how they're different—and about how people feel about their differences. Children take their cues from the adults they love. You make such a wonderful difference in children's attitudes when you offer an atmosphere of acceptance.

One of life's joys is discovering that we can be open to new experiences that at first seem strange or even scary. It's exhilarating to find that the barriers that seem to separate us from other people begin to vanish when we take the time to get to know those people. That's the way it is with real friends.

Fred Rogers

There are all sorts of people in the world, and every one of us is different. That's something that makes everyone special.

Even though we're different in some ways,

we are also alike in many ways. We all want to
love and be loved.

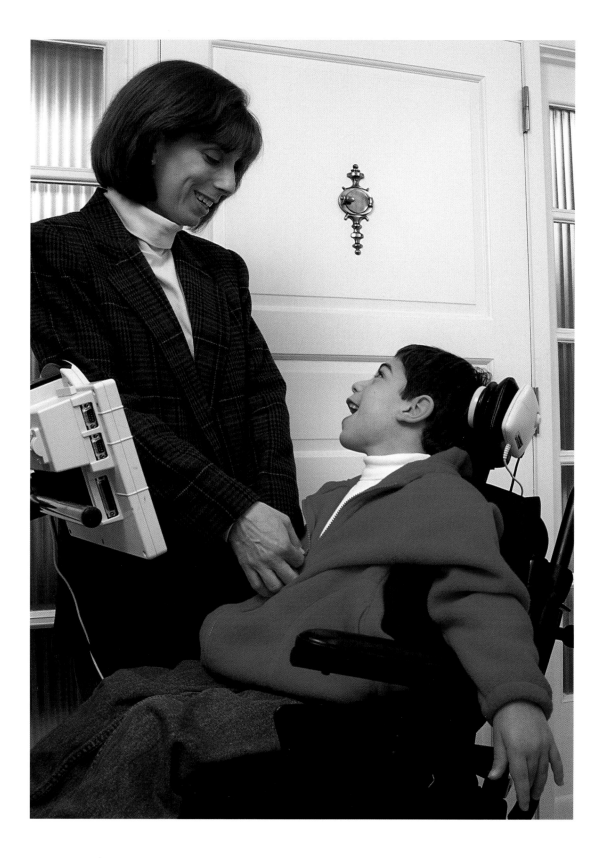

Sometimes it can be hard to remember how much people are alike, especially when you meet someone who doesn't walk or talk or learn the same way you do. You might be curious. Sometimes you might have questions . . .

and other times you might not.

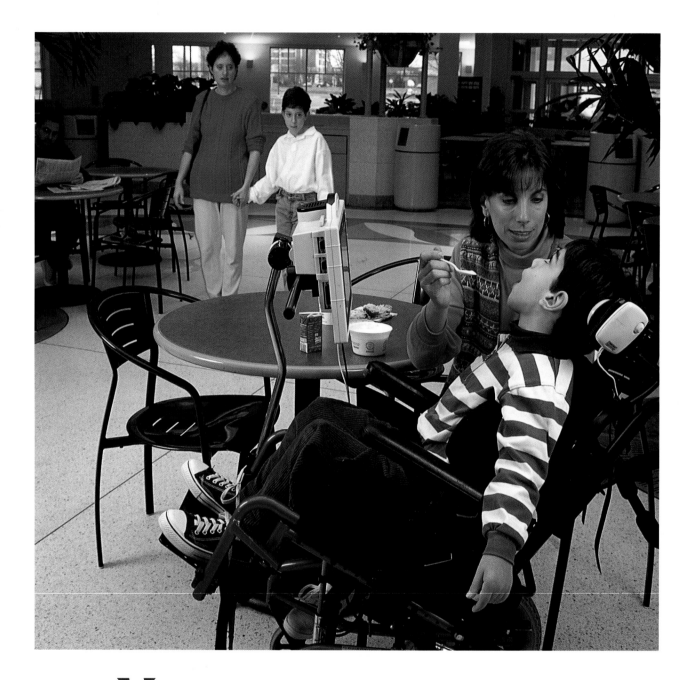

You could even be surprised when you see something you don't expect. Or you might feel afraid when someone does something you don't expect.

You might wonder, "Why is he like that?" or "What happened to him?" You might want to know about some everyday things like, "How does he eat or get dressed or what does he like to do?"

It can help to talk about whatever you're wondering and feeling with the grownups in your family or at school. They may not know the answers to all your questions. Nobody can know everything, but they may be able to help you find a comfortable way to learn about what you want to know.

If you would like to meet someone, you could start by saying, "Hi!" and telling each other your names. Most people like to know you're interested in them. Your questions could be really important to them.

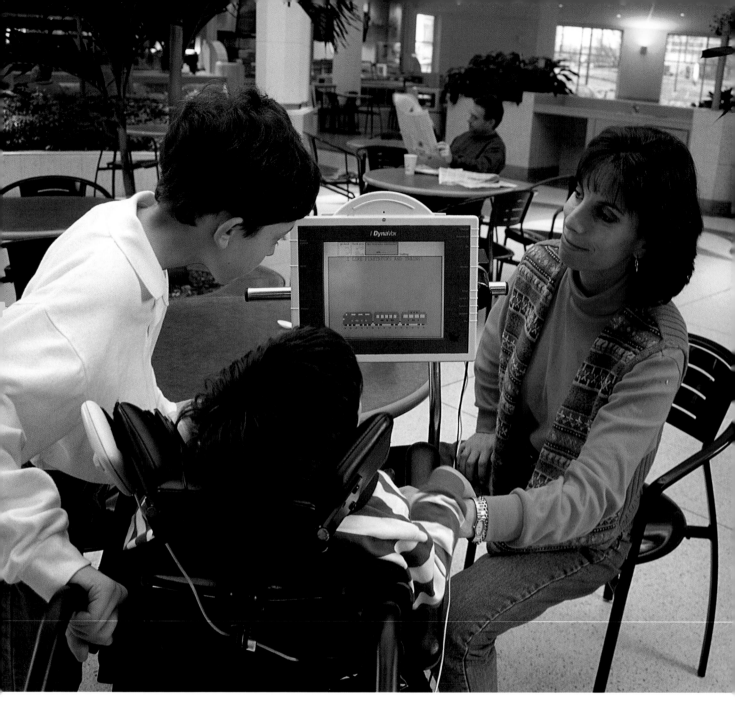

People who can't talk may be able to let you know about themselves in other ways.

You might want to find out more about the things people use to help them, like their wheelchairs or walkers.

If you feel like trying to help somebody, it's a good idea to ask first. Sometimes people want help, and sometimes they don't.

Isn't it that way for you, too? Sometimes you want help, and sometimes you want to try to do things on your own.

When you know more about someone,
you might find that there are things you
both like . . .

_____

things you want to do together . . .

and things you can learn from each other.

There are things you can do to help each other . . .

and things you can tell each other, even hard
things, such as "I don't like when you do that."

Good friends can be truthful with each other.

There are lots of fun things that you can laugh about together.

The more you know about someone, the more you understand that person.

We all need people who love us and who care for us. That's true for everybody.

Everybody needs friends.

As you grow, you'll find there's so much to learn about people . . . so much more than what you see when you first meet them. And getting to know other people can help you learn more about yourself, too.

You are special . . . and so is everyone else in the world.

Special thanks to:
Hedda Bluestone Sharapan for research and development.
Our friends at the Center for Children and Families at the Educational
Development Center, Inc., Boston, Massachusetts;
Mara Kaplan at the Center for Creative Play, Pittsburgh, Pennsylvania;
Claudia Lep and Zoena Rader at MOSAIC;
our friends at LEAP Pittsburgh;
Margaret Kimmel, Ph.D., University of Pittsburgh School of Information Sciences;
Al Condeluci, Ph.D., United Cerebral Palsy of Pittsburgh;
Bonnie Utley, Ph.D., University of Colorado at Denver, School of Education,
Program in Special Education;
Jordan Nance and his good friend Justin Bedell;
The Carnegie Library of Pittsburgh, Homewood Branch;
The Carnegie Museum of Natural History;
The Carnegie Science Center;
Phipps Conservatory and Botanical Gardens;
The Port Authority of Allegheny County;
South Hills Village.

And an extra special thanks to the families and friends who so graciously
gave their time and enthusiasm to appear in the photographs.

Project Director: Margy Whitmer.
Designed by Marikka Tamura. Text set in Lucida Bright.
Library of Congress Cataloging-in-Publication Data
Rogers, Fred. Extraordinary friends / Fred Rogers ; photographs by Jim Judkis.
p. cm. — (Let's talk about it) Summary: Focuses on people who have disabilities, who might use
equipment such as wheelchairs or special computers, who are more like you than you might think,
and suggests ways to interact with them. 1. Handicapped children Juvenile literature.
[1. Handicapped.] I. Judkis, Jim, ill. II. Title. III. Series: Rogers, Fred. Let's talk about it.
HV888.R63 2000 362.4'083—DC21 99-17615 CIP
ISBN 0-698-11861-8 (pbk)
ISBN 0-399-23146-3 (hc)
3 5 7 9 10 8 6 4 2